Table c

EINDHOVEN
TRAVEL GUIDE

Unlock Hidden Gems, Must-See
Sights, Culture, Adventures, and
Thrilling Experiences

CORI J. SMITH

Copyright© Cori J. Smith 2023

INTRODUCTION

Greetings from the dynamic city of Eindhoven, where culture and innovation blend to create a singular tapestry of experiences. Located in the center of the Netherlands, Eindhoven is a center for innovation, design, and history that is just waiting to be discovered.

The striking fusion of modern architecture with old-world charm may be the first thing that draws your attention to Eindhoven. Its transformation from an industrial powerhouse to a bustling metropolis is illustrated by the cityscape. It's normal to feel in awe of the magnificent buildings that make up Eindhoven's skyline.

Located roughly at 51.4416° N latitude and 5.4697° E longitude, Eindhoven is more than simply a place to visit; it's an adventure waiting to happen. Eindhoven is regarded as the "City of Light" in honor of its distinguished past as the home of the Philips Company, a pioneer in the electronics industry.

The history of Eindhoven begins in the 13th century when a tiny village grew up around the meeting point of the Dommel and Gender rivers. The name of the city, Eindhoven, is a combination of the words "hoven," which denotes a settlement, and "eind," which means "last" or "end." After being granted city powers in 1232, Eindhoven, which had previously been a hamlet, gradually expanded into a town.

The quaint De Bergen neighborhood is home to surviving examples of the medieval buildings that laced the city's historical fabric. Discover the 15th-century Gothic splendor of St. Catherine's

Church at Kerkstraat 1, nestled amidst the cobblestone streets. Its imposing spire beckons, providing a window into the religious history of the city.

In the late 1800s, Eindhoven saw an industrial revolution, spurred on by the founding of the Philips Company in 1891. This electrical behemoth not only influenced the destiny of the city but also had a major influence on the advancement of electronics worldwide. Visit the Philips Museum located at Emmasingel 31 to learn about the development of this innovative business.

Eindhoven was at the core of Operation Market Garden during World War II. Due to the city's strategic importance, Allied forces were able to liberate it in September 1944; this event is remembered at the 18 Septemberplein square. The 'Wings of Liberation' monument marks the start of the Liberation Route, which leads you through significant locations and tells the story of the city during the war.

An age of invention and design was ushered in by post-war reconstruction. See this change for yourself at Strijp-S, the creative hub that was once the Philips industrial complex. Explore this area, which is bursting at the seams with hip stores, art exhibits, and a lively vibe. Eindhoven's metamorphosis from an industrial heavyweight to a design-focused city is perfectly captured by Strijp-S.

To fully understand Eindhoven's past, one must pay a visit to the DAF Museum located at Tongelresestraat 27. An essential component of the city's automotive heritage is DAF, which was established in 1928. The museum features an amazing assortment of vehicles, trucks, and inventions.

The city is full of creative and innovative people, as demonstrated by the Design Academy Eindhoven, located at 11 Emmasingel. Since its founding in 1955, this institution has served as a breeding ground for creative designers. Take a look at the innovative designs and concepts influencing the direction of design by visiting on weekdays between 9 AM and 5 PM.

At Noord Brabantlaan 1a, wander along the Evoluon's illuminated trail as the sun sets over Eindhoven. Constructed in 1966, this futuristic building with a flying saucer-like appearance functioned as a science and technology museum. Its outside remains an architectural monument to Eindhoven's progressive spirit, even though its interior is no longer open.

The vibrant current of Eindhoven is inextricably linked to the city's illustrious past. Every area of Eindhoven has a tale to tell, whether you're following in the footsteps of the Middle Ages, discovering industrial landmarks, or getting lost in modern architecture. So, explorers, let the ghosts of the past lead you as you discover this dynamic city where the past and present coexist together.

So, dear visitors, let yourself be opened to the vibrant energy of Eindhoven as you set out on your tour. Eindhoven greets you with open arms and promises a tapestry of experiences that will remain in your memories for years to come, from cutting-edge technology to enthralling culture. I hope you have fun exploring this amazing city!

Chapter 1

GETTING TO KNOW EINDHOVEN

Geography and Location

Greetings from Eindhoven, a city well positioned in the southern region of the Netherlands, roughly located at 51.4416° N latitude and 5.4697° E longitude. The accessibility and cultural significance of Eindhoven within the nation are greatly influenced by its geographical position.

Nestled at the meeting point of the Dommel and Gender rivers, in the province of North Brabant, Eindhoven presents a magnificent scene that combines natural beauty with urban refinement. Travelers visiting the Netherlands will find the city to be an easy hub due to its central location throughout the nation.

The city center of Eindhoven is a patchwork of pleasant squares and meandering streets, each of which reveals a different aspect of the city's vibrant modern past. Notable sites to see when exploring the city include the Gothic-styled St. Catherine's Church at Kerkstraat 1, which serves as an anchor for the city's historical center. Situated at Tongelresestraat 27, the DAF Museum is a noteworthy attraction that adds to the city's rich automotive history. Both venues are conveniently located in the center of Eindhoven.

It is impossible to talk about the geography of Eindhoven without mentioning the Strijp-S district. This urban site, a former industrial complex turned bustling center of culture and the arts, epitomizes Eindhoven's dynamic development. Strijp-S is an example of how well the city repurposes spaces, and the vibrant environment there reflects current urban life.

Within the city, Genneper Parken offers a natural haven for those in need of some peace. Situated in Antoon Coolenlaan 1, this vast park is home to several recreational amenities, such as a swimming pool and an outdoor museum dedicated to historical events, in addition to being a verdant haven.

Discovering Eindhoven's topography will reveal that the city's design promotes bicycling and walking, allowing guests to easily become fully immersed in the culture. So, my dear travelers, while you discover the marvels this city has to offer, let its geography serve as your guide.

Climate and Best Time to Visit

Let's now discuss the weather in Eindhoven, which has a big impact on how much you enjoy your trip. The climate in Eindhoven is temperate maritime, with pleasant summers and generally mild winters.

To make the most of your time at this alluring location, organize your vacation with an understanding of the city's climate.

The summer months of June through August are without a doubt the busiest for travel to Eindhoven. The city comes to life with festivals, outdoor activities, and a positive vibe. The pleasant 20–25°C (68–77°F) daytime temperatures make it the perfect time to explore the city's outdoor attractions, such as the bustling Stratumseind nightlife zone.

Take into consideration traveling in the shoulder seasons of spring (March to May) or fall (September to November) if you want more comfortable weather and fewer tourists. Eindhoven enjoys nice weather throughout these months, with temperatures between 10°C and 20°C (50°F and 68°F). It's a great time to take in the blossoming flowers in city parks or take a stroll around the historical neighborhoods away from the bustle of peak season.

In Eindhoven, winter lasts from December to February. The average temperature during this time is between 0 and 8°C (32 and 46°F). Even though the city experiences mild winters in comparison to other European destinations, the city comes alive with seasonal markets and spectacular lighting. This may be the ideal time of year for you to visit if you like more intimate city experiences and wintertime activities.

It's important to remember that, like much of the Netherlands, Eindhoven can see rainy seasons all year round. Consequently, regardless of the season, it is important to bring an umbrella or raincoat. Remember, Dutch people are used to riding in all kinds of weather, so rain or shine, renting a bike may still be a fun way to get around.

When it comes to events, think about scheduling your trip around either the Glow Eindhoven Light Festival in November or Dutch Design Week in October. These festivities heighten the excitement of the event and highlight the city's creative energy.

In conclusion, your tastes will determine the ideal time to visit Eindhoven. Throughout the year, Eindhoven invites visitors seeking the vibrant energy of summer, the peace of shoulder seasons, or the magic of winter celebrations. So prepare to immerse yourself in the distinct charm of this Dutch jewel by packing appropriately.

Local Customs and Etiquette

Salutations, fellow explorers! To guarantee a smooth and courteous visit to this dynamic Dutch city, you must acquaint yourself with the customs and etiquette of the area before setting off on your adventure through Eindhoven.

Let's start by discussing the Dutch greeting customs. A cordial "Hallo" (hello) is a typical and widely recognized greeting. While professional settings need handshakes, friends, and acquaintances can get by with a simple verbal greeting or a casual nod. Remember that the Dutch are renowned for their straightforward

14

communication style; they don't like to mince words and cherish honesty.

Bicycles are commonplace throughout the city, especially in the core region at 51.4416° N latitude and 5.4697° E longitude. Bikers love Eindhoven, and the people here take their two-wheelers very seriously. Be mindful of bike lanes when you're strolling; they're denoted by red pavement or signage. Never assume a Dutch cyclist is going to go fast, and always look both ways before crossing these lanes!

Let's now discuss the Dutch notion of "gezelligheid." This phrase, which is difficult to translate, connotes coziness, warmth, and a friendly vibe. This spirit is evident in the cafes of Eindhoven, where residents congregate for a leisurely lunch or a cup of coffee. To fully embrace this tradition, take your time sipping your drink, striking up a discussion, and relishing the occasion.

Tipping is not required when dining, however, it is traditional. Tipping between 5 and 10% is customary in dining establishments, whereas at cafes, it's customary to round up the amount. In contrast to certain cultures, service fees are usually included in the price; nonetheless, a small gratuity for exceptional service is always appreciated.

You may come into the Dutch custom of "gezellig uitgaan," or socializing, when out and about in the city. An ideal location for this is the Stratumseind, one of the Netherlands' longest bar streets. Enjoying the nightlife around 51.4399° N latitude and 5.4828° E longitude? Be aware that hours of operation can change, however most places close at 2 AM. Drinks are usually purchased in rounds, and it's courteous to accept an offer to purchase a drink from someone else.

In Dutch society, personal space is highly valued. Unless you are familiar with someone, keep a comfortable space during talks and refrain from making physical contact like kissing or hugging. The Dutch respect private and are appreciative of others who share such values.

Let's now talk about the Dutch dedication to sustainability. Recycling bins can be found all across the city of Eindhoven, which supports environmentally responsible practices. Participate in the endeavor by sorting your rubbish and remembering to use less water and energy wherever you go.

A trip to St. Catherine's Church at Kerkstraat 1 offers you a taste of religious tradition as you delve into Eindhoven's cultural landscape. Religious locations should be treated with respect, so please don't make excessive noise and abide by any set rules.

You might come across avant-garde installations and artworks in the vibrant Strijp-S neighborhood, a creative and cultural hotspot. Even while the environment invites investigation, keep in mind to respect public areas and refrain from touching or tampering with exhibits unless permitted to do so.

Immerse yourself in the festivities while keeping an eye on your surroundings when you visit events or festivals like the Glow Eindhoven Light Festival or the Dutch Design Week. Respect the diversity of participants and viewers and abide by the rules unique to the event.

Lastly, keep in mind that haggling is not customary in the Netherlands while you peruse the neighborhood markets and boutiques. Since prices are usually set, trying to haggle may be viewed as strange or rude. Rather, savor the shopping encounter and seize the chance to interact with regional craftspeople.

In conclusion, the manners and customs of Eindhoven are a reflection of the Dutch ideals of integrity, deference to private property, and enjoyment of a gezellig ambiance. Adopting these habits will help you not only get around the city with ease but also add to the friendly and upbeat atmosphere that characterizes Eindhoven. So, my dear visitors, as you set out on an enlightening adventure around this fascinating Dutch city, let the local customs serve as your compass!

Chapter 2

ESSENTIAL TRAVEL INFORMATION

Transportation Guide

Greetings from the center of the Eindhoven transit system, my beloved travelers. Having the correct information at your fingertips makes navigating  a city easy. Let's get started with the Eindhoven transit guide to make sure your trip around this vibrant Dutch city goes well and without incident.

Getting In:

Thanks to Eindhoven Airport (EIN), a modern airport, the city has excellent international connections. The airport is conveniently located at Luchthavenweg 25, about 5 kilometers west of the city center, and is easily accessible by several different means of transportation.

Eindhoven Airport serves both domestic and international flights and provides a gateway to the city and its environs for those coming by air. It's easy to get to the city center from the airport.

The most practical choice is the shuttle bus, which is appropriately called "Bus 400 Eindhoven." The bus travels to the central station immediately from the airport, arriving in about twenty minutes. Tickets cost about €3.75 for a one-way ride, and they can be bought from the bus driver or at the airport.

Taxis are easily accessible outside the airport terminal for individuals who would rather travel a straight path. Depending on the specific destination, a taxi ride to the city center takes about fifteen minutes and costs about twenty-five euros. Before beginning your trip, always get the driver to confirm the fare.

You'll be happy to hear that Eindhoven Airport promotes environmental awareness if you're an advocate for environmentally friendly travel. The airport is dedicated to environmentally friendly projects, and this includes electric buses and electric car charging stations.

Getting Around the City:

After arriving in Eindhoven, you can enjoy a delightful exploration of the city because of its well-organized and varied transportation network.

- Public Transportation: Buses make up the majority of Eindhoven's first-rate public transportation system. Eindhoven Central Station, situated at Stationsplein 22, serves as the main bus hub. Buses branch out to all areas of the city and beyond from this hub. If you plan to take public transportation, you might think about getting an OV-chipkaart, a smart card that can be loaded with credit and used on all

Dutch public transportation systems. Alternatively, tickets for a single voyage can be purchased straight from the bus driver.

- Biking: Discover Eindhoven on two wheels and embrace the local way of life. Here, biking is a way of life rather than merely a means of transportation. Affordable daily or weekly rentals are available from several bike rental companies, including Fietsenstalling Bike Shop at Smalle Haven 123. Riding a bike through the city is safe and fun because of the network of designated bike lanes.

- Walking: Eindhoven's city center is made for pedestrians, so exploring on foot is the best way to take in all of its delights. Many sights are within reasonable walking distance, from the fashionable Strijp-S neighborhood to the old St. Catherine's Church at Kerkstraat 1. As you stroll around the charming squares and streets, comfortable shoes are the ideal traveling companion.

- Renting a car offers flexibility to people who want to travel outside of their local borders. Numerous cars are available for rent from companies like Enterprise Rent-A-Car at Hugo van der Goeslaan 1. It's important to use approved parking spots or park-and-ride facilities because parking in the city center may be limited.

- Taxi Services: Taxis are a convenient door-to-door transportation alternative, and they are available all around the city. You can find designated taxi stands or hail a cab on the street. TCA Eindhoven Taxi and Eindhoven Taxi Services are two well-known taxi businesses. Before beginning your trip, always get the driver to confirm the fare. Electric taxis are becoming more and more common in the city, which takes pride in its dedication to sustainability. It's an environmentally responsible way to see Eindhoven in addition to being convenient.

- Electric Scooters: Take a look at electric scooters for an enjoyable and environmentally responsible way to cruise the city. Companies that provide electric scooter rentals include Check and Felyx. Just download the app, find a scooter that is close by, and get going. Remember to abide by authorized parking places and local traffic laws.

Navigating Eindhoven's Streets:

Being aware of the layout of the city's streets enhances your enjoyment of your explorations. With attractions like the lively Markt Square and the Van Abbemuseum at 2 Bilderdijklaan, the city center is a center of activity. Expect a blend of industrial and modern architecture as you explore Strijp-S; there are cafes, boutiques, and cultural venues just waiting to be explored.

St. Catherine's Church towers over the De Bergen neighborhood, which offers a glimpse into Eindhoven's past. With its green spaces and recreational amenities, Genneper Parken, which is situated at Antoon Coolenlaan 1, provides a tranquil haven.

Whether you like the ease and convenience of public transit, the cultural diversity of biking, or the independence of self-exploration by automobile, Eindhoven's transportation system is made to accommodate all tastes.

Ultimately, as you navigate the city using its various transit choices, let the trip itself become a part of your experience in Eindhoven. Every way to get about this vibrant Dutch city, whether you're zooming into it from Eindhoven Airport or cruising along its bike lanes, shows a new aspect. So, my dear travelers, enjoy the variety of possibilities available to you and let Eindhoven's discovery reveal itself to you!

Public Transport System

Salutations, fellow travelers! The public transportation system in Eindhoven is your pass to an easy and quick trip throughout this vibrant Dutch city. To make sure you can easily navigate the city, let's go on a guided tour of the main features of Eindhoven's public transportation system.

Buses: The vast bus network in Eindhoven is the lifeblood of the city's public transportation system. Eindhoven Central Station, a transportation hub at 22 Stationsplein, is the hub of this system. Buses leave from this location and travel to different parts of the city and its environs.

If you want to take the bus, you might think about purchasing an OV-chipkaart, a smart card that makes traveling easier. You can load it with credit and use it to swipe on and out of buses, trams, and trains all around the Netherlands without any problems. Single voyage tickets are available for purchase straight from the bus driver for infrequent travelers.

A single travel ticket costs between €2.50 and €4.00, depending on where you want to go in the city. Alternatively, for about €6.00, you might get a day pass that allows you unlimited travel within Eindhoven, which is a more economical option.

Numerous locations are served by the bus lines, which link well-known sites like the Van Abbemuseum at 2 Bilderdijklaan to the hip Strijp-S neighborhood. The bus system is a dependable travel companion, whether you're a history buff visiting St. Catherine's Church at Kerkstraat 1 or a cultural vulture going to the Design Academy Eindhoven at 11 Emmasingel.

Trains: In addition to serving as a bus terminal, Eindhoven Central Station is a significant train hub that links the city to locations throughout the world. From this hub, regional, high-speed, and transcontinental trains run smoothly, offering quick and easy access to cities like Rotterdam, Utrecht, and Amsterdam.

The railway station, furnished with necessary amenities including ticket booths and information kiosks, guarantees a seamless transfer between various forms of transportation. The price of a train ticket varies depending on where you're going, whether you're going on a day trip or seeing neighboring Dutch cities. A one-way ticket to Amsterdam Central, for example, can cost anything between €20 and €30.

Travel Cards and Subscriptions: Take into account the convenience of travel cards or subscriptions if you travel frequently or are planning a longer stay. These alternatives offer flexibility and the possibility of cost savings, and they are available for varying durations. They are available at the central station or on the official websites of transit agencies.

About €6.00 gets you unlimited bus riding inside Eindhoven for a day. Consider purchasing a regional travel pass, which can cost between €15 and €20 per day and provide you access to buses and trains in the surrounding area, if you plan to explore outside of the city limits.

Travel Advice: A few suggestions can improve your trip and help you get the most out of using public transportation. Use internet resources or smartphone apps to stay up to current on schedules in real-time. Pay attention to busy times, especially in the morning and evening when there may be more people using public transportation.

The public transportation system in Eindhoven offers a tour through the city's lively neighborhoods, notable historical sites, and cultural hubs in addition to a means of transportation from point A to point B. So get on board and allow public transportation in Eindhoven to take you around the rich diversity of the city.

Biking Culture in Eindhoven

Prepare to pedal through the center of the dynamic bike culture of Eindhoven - an experience that embodies a way of life and transcends just transportation. Come along as we delve into the specifics of Eindhoven's bike culture, covering everything from bike rentals to getting a feel for this city's daily routine.

Renting Bikes: Visit one of the several bike rental stores located throughout the city to fully immerse yourself in Eindhoven's bicycling culture. Fietsenstalling Bike Shop at Smalle Haven 123 is a noteworthy choice; they provide a variety of bikes, from electric to tandem, to suit all tastes and levels of cycling experience. Bicycle rentals are easy to arrange and provide you the flexibility to see the city at your speed.

Depending on the kind of bike you select, a day's rental might cost anywhere from €10 to €15. An easy and environmentally responsible method to get around the city, electric bikes can be a little more expensive, typically ranging from €20 to €25 per day.

Cycling Infrastructure: With a system of designated bike lanes winding across the city, Eindhoven takes great pleasure in its cycling infrastructure. These designated lanes, which are frequently isolated from oncoming traffic, offer a convenient and secure path across the streets of Eindhoven. All levels of cyclists can enjoy the enhanced cycling experience provided by the level terrain.

You'll observe the city's dedication to making biking a pleasurable and stress-free pastime as you bike through Eindhoven. There are lots of bike racks in handy places in well-known locations like the central station, marketplaces, and performance spaces.

Joining the Locals: Go on a daily bike ride with the locals to experience Eindhoven's bike culture. The city center is transformed into a vibrant mosaic of bikers, including families taking leisurely rides, professionals making their way to work, and students on their way to classes.

Feel free to adopt the Dutch style of bicycling, which is laid-back, sensible, and frequently accompanied by a feeling of gezelligheid, or a warm and welcoming atmosphere.

Participating in the city's bicycling culture offers a stronger connection to its lifestyle in addition to a unique viewpoint of the city.

Cycling Events: The city of Eindhoven celebrates its passion for bicycling with several events and initiatives that go beyond daily commutes. Look out for cycling-related events and activities, such as community bike tours and group rides. These events allow visitors to meet residents and learn about the various facets of Eindhoven's bike culture.

Safety and manners: Bicycling is a common and entertaining sport, but safety comes first at all times. It is advisable to wear a helmet when traveling outside of the city core. Observe traffic laws, give way to pedestrians, and indicate your intentions with your hands. When not in use, lock your bike securely using one of the accessible bike racks.

In summary, the city of Eindhoven's riding culture is a way of life that the people there have embraced rather than merely a means of transportation. So grab a bike, enjoy the wind in your hair, and ride through the quaint neighborhoods and welcoming streets of Eindhoven to become a member of the city's cycling community. Allow your bike's beat to synchronize with the city's pulse, generating experiences and memories that transcend simple conveyance. Happy riding!

Chapter 3

ACCOMMODATION OPTIONS

Hotels, Hostels, and Unique Stays

Greetings, cherished tourists, from the world of lodging in Eindhoven, where your visit becomes an essential component of your journey. Eindhoven has accommodations to suit every preference and budget, whether you're looking for the coziness of a hostel, the excitement of a novel stay, or both. Let's investigate the variety of choices this fascinating Dutch city has to offer.

Hotels: A Comfortable Haven

There are several hotels in Eindhoven, and each one offers a special combination of convenience and comfort. The Pullman Eindhoven Cocagne, located at Vestdijk 47, is one noteworthy choice. This posh hotel is tucked away in the center of the city and offers contemporary rooms with chic decor to make sure you have a sumptuous getaway. The hotel offers facilities like a rooftop pool, a fitness facility, and an on-site restaurant that takes guests on a delightful gastronomic adventure. Typically, rooms start around €150 per night.

The Inntel Hotels Art Eindhoven in Lichttoren 22 beckons to people who enjoy historical charm. This four-star hotel, which used to be a Philips factory, effortlessly combines modern elegance with industrial aesthetics. The hotel is a visual treat because of its distinctive architecture and creative flair. Rates for a single night start at about €120, making this a reasonably priced yet fashionable lodging choice.

The Hotel La Reine, at Wilhelminaplein 3, offers a warm ambiance in the heart of the city if you'd rather be in a more private environment. This boutique hotel offers uniquely decorated rooms, each with a distinct personality, making for a unique and endearing stay. The usual price range for a night is between €90 and €120.

Hostels: Budget-Friendly and Sociable

Budget-conscious tourists looking for a friendly environment can find a warm embrace at Eindhoven's hostels. One excellent example is the Blue Collar Hotel, which is located at Klokgebouw 10. Located in the well-known Strijp-S neighborhood, this hostel offers both private rooms and shared dorms with an industrial feel. A dynamic social atmosphere is fostered by the community rooms, which include an outdoor terrace and a lively bar. Dormitory beds are an inexpensive option for individuals who prioritize low-cost lodging without compromising style, with rates starting at about €25 per night.

The SLEEP-INN Eindhoven at Leenderweg 47 provides a warm and welcoming environment for those looking for a more central location. This hostel offers a variety of lodging options, including private rooms and shared dormitories, and is well-maintained with a unique decor and welcoming staff. Dormitory beds are a great option for tourists on a limited budget, with prices starting at about €20 per night.

Unique Stays: Where Quirk Meets Comfort

For individuals seeking an unparalleled experience, Eindhoven has a range of distinctive lodging options that guarantee to enhance your voyage. Situated in Paradijslaan 2-8, the Kazerne Hotel seamlessly blends design, art, and hospitality. Situated in a former military barracks, this boutique hotel boasts rooms furnished with modern artwork and design elements. For those who enjoy both cuisine and art, the on-site restaurant is a refuge that features innovative cooking. Prices for rooms begin at €200 per night.

Experience the 'Starry Night' at Daalakkersweg 2, the Van Gogh-Roosegaarde Cycle Path, for a getaway that combines nature and modernity. This cycling route has reactive lighting that imitates the night sky and was inspired by the well-known painting by Van Gogh. It's not your typical lodging, but it does provide a unique evening experience. The bike route is free to access and offers a magical experience beneath the sky.

Tips & Considerations for Booking

Here are some suggestions to improve your booking experience, regardless of whether you choose a hotel, hostel, or a distinctive stay:

- Online Reservations: Through their official websites or reliable booking platforms, the majority of Eindhoven lodgings provide online booking alternatives. It's best to book your accommodations well in advance, particularly during the busiest travel times.

- Seasonal Rates: Depending on the season, lodging costs can change. If you want to travel during the shoulder seasons, you can find cheaper lodging and nicer weather.

- Package Deals: Look into packages that can include travel, lodging, and/or dining. These packages may offer further benefits and financial savings.

- Facilities and Reviews: Examine the accommodations' facilities and read guest reviews to gain a sense of the whole experience before confirming your reservation.

- Location: Take into account how your lodging will relate to the activities you have scheduled. Remaining in the center makes it simple to get to major transportation hubs and attractions.

Let your choice of lodging improve your entire experience when you pick your home away from home in Eindhoven. All of the accommodations—the plushness of a hotel, the community of a hostel, or the distinctiveness of a themed stay—contribute to the colorful fabric of your travel experience. So, my dear visitors, may your lodging of choice turn into a warm haven, guaranteeing that your stay in Eindhoven becomes more than just a visit—rather, it becomes a memorable part of your journey.

Neighborhood Guide for Choosing Accommodation in Eindhoven

Greetings from Eindhoven, a city full of varied areas, each with its distinct personality and allure. Let's explore Eindhoven's various neighborhoods together as you set out to discover the ideal lodging, assisting you in selecting a location that best suits your tastes and vacation objectives.

City Center: Vibrant and Historic Elegance

The City Center, the pulsating heart of Eindhoven, is distinguished by its lively squares, ancient buildings, and energetic ambiance. Wander around the picturesque alleyways around Markt Square or stroll down the lively Stratumseind, which is well-known for its exciting nightlife.

The City Center is home to a variety of hotels, from boutique establishments like Hotel La Reine to opulent choices like the Pullman Eindhoven Cocagne, all of which are close to important sites like St. Catherine's Church and the Van Abbemuseum.

Strijp-S: Creativity and Innovation

Strijp-S, a formerly industrial neighborhood turned creative center, is renowned for its hip atmosphere, cutting-edge architecture, and creative flair. This neighborhood is home to unique culinary establishments, independent stores, and art installations.

Accommodations: Strijp-S is a great option for people looking for a modern and vibrant ambiance. Standout accommodations include the industrial-chic Blue Collar Hotel and the unique Kazerne Hotel.

De Bergen: Quaint and Charming

Cobblestone streets, quaint cafes, and boutique stores abound in the charming district of De Bergen. This neighborhood has a bohemian vibe and is ideal for people who value a relaxed and creative atmosphere.

Accommodations: Within walking distance of De Bergen's lovely squares and artistic centers are charming hotels such as the Hotel Marienhage and boutique guesthouses, providing a quiet haven.

Woensel: Community Spirit and Local Living

Important Features: Woensel offers a window into local life as a varied and residential neighborhood. Savor a variety of green spaces, retail avenues, and traditional Dutch marketplaces. The location provides a more sedate atmosphere, although it's still close to the city center.

Accommodations: SLEEP-INN Eindhoven is an affordable choice that offers a comfortable stay along with convenient access to local markets and community activities.

Tongelre: Calm Suburban Living

Tongelre provides a peaceful, family-friendly suburban haven with parks and green areas. Perfect for those looking for a quiet getaway away from the bustle of the city but with easy access to Eindhoven's top attractions.

Accommodations: If you're looking for a quiet getaway close to Tongelre's parks and natural areas, consider staying at hotels on the outskirts like the NH Collection Eindhoven Centre.

Gestel: Luxurious Living

With tree-lined streets and a blend of modern and old architecture, Gestel is renowned for its residential charm. This neighborhood offers a peaceful environment with quick access to parks and cultural events.

Accommodations: For a chic stay close to Gestel's elegant surroundings, choose hotels of a higher caliber, like the Inntel Hotels Art Eindhoven.

Tips for Selecting a Place to Stay:

- Transportation: If you intend to venture outside of your surrounding neighborhood, find out how close your selected lodging is to public transportation hubs.

- Budget: Various neighborhoods have a variety of lodging choices to accommodate a range of spending levels. Find the ideal balance between cost and comfort by taking your financial preferences into account.
- Interests: Decide which neighborhood best suits your hobbies. Eindhoven's neighborhoods provide a variety of experiences, including nightlife, art and culture, and peaceful seclusion.
- Accessibility: Make sure your area of choice has easy access to any attractions or activities you have in mind.
- Local Experience: For a genuine Dutch experience, choose neighborhoods like Woensel or Tongelre if you want to immerse yourself in the local way of life.

In summary, every district in Eindhoven has a distinct history, and your lodging selection will influence that history. Whichever district you choose—the bustling City Center, the artistic vibrancy of Strijp-S, or the rustic charm of Tongelre—each provides a unique setting for your

Eindhoven experience. So, my dear tourists, may the neighborhood you have selected serve as the blank canvas on which to paint your memories of Eindhoven, weaving a tale of experiences that accurately capture the spirit of this fascinating city in the Netherlands.

Chapter 4

UNVEILING HIDDEN GEMS

Off-the-Beaten-Path Attractions in Eindhoven

Greetings from the lesser-known treasures and hidden gems of Eindhoven, inquisitive tourists. Beyond the well-traveled roads are interesting sights that give your visit to Eindhoven a dash of intrigue and originality. Let's take a trip to explore six lesser-known gems in the city that are off the typical tourist route.

The Hidden Gardens of Philips de Jongh Park

Location: Frederiklaan, Philips de Jongh Park, Eindhoven

Philips de Jongh Park has several secret gardens tucked away that provide a tranquil haven from the hustle and bustle of the city. Take a stroll around these well-kept green spaces, each with its distinct atmosphere and vegetation. Explore undiscovered sculptures, charming bridges, and serene areas ideal for reflection.

Evoluon: Iconic Architecture and Innovation

Location: Noord Brabantlaan 1A, Evoluon, Eindhoven.

Evoluon is not a complete unknown, but it stays out of the spotlight a lot. This famous building, which has a UFO-like appearance, is proof of Eindhoven's inventiveness. Originally constructed as a museum of technology, it currently holds exhibitions and activities. See their schedule for exclusive events, such as tech demos and cultural gatherings.

Step into the Past at 't Oude Wandelpark

Location: Alberdingk Thijmlaan, Eindhoven's 't Oude Wandelpark.

Translated as "The Old Walking Park," 't Oude Wandelpark is a picturesque green area rich in history. Wander the walkways surrounded by trees, come across historic monuments, and discover peace in this little-known haven. Bring a picnic, relax by the pond, and take in this hidden park's ageless beauty.

Experience Art and Nature at Ton Smits Huis

Location: Hemelrijken 6, Ton Smits Huis, Eindhoven.

Tucked away in a residential area, Ton Smits Huis is a charming fusion of art and environment. Cartoonist Ton Smits's wacky sculptures and constructions are on display in this former residence. His artwork adorning the surrounding landscape provides a magical environment. You can immerse yourself in this exceptional artistic refuge for free.

Stratumse Heide: Tranquil Heathland

Location: Eindhoven, Stratumse Heide, Aalsterweg.

Get away from the bustle of the city and discover the tranquil Stratumse Heide. This vast heathland offers peace and natural beauty within a short distance from the city. Take in the clean, fresh air as you stroll around the walking trails, and take in the expansive, heather-dotted scenery. It's the perfect location for a tranquil getaway amid the wilderness.

Explore Berenkuil's Urban Art Gallery

Location: Eindhoven's Berenkuil, Insulindelaan

Explore Berenkuil, an outdoor gallery converted from a traffic circle, the artistic underbelly of Eindhoven. This unusual location, adorned with colorful murals and street art, serves as a canvas for regional and global artists. Discover the constantly changing exhibits that transform a basic roundabout into a vibrant display of urban art.

Lesser-Known Neighborhoods to Explore

The allure of Eindhoven is beyond its well-known neighborhoods. Explore the less well-known neighborhoods; each has a distinct charm, history, and personality. Let's explore six undiscovered treasures that claim to provide a closer-knit and more genuine look into the heart of the city.

Lively Vibes in De Hurk: Though it may not be marked on many travel guides, De Hurk is a vibrant industrial district. From obscure cafes to neighborhood markets, it's a microcosm of the varied cultures of Eindhoven. On game days, take in the vibrant atmosphere at PSV Eindhoven's home stadium, the Philips Stadion.

The charm of History at Begijnenhof: Begijnenhof is a historical jewel that is nestled away close to the city core.

Reminiscent of Eindhoven's past, this peaceful hamlet boasts charming courtyards and well-preserved architecture. Explore its winding streets and take in this undiscovered neighborhood's serene beauty.

Diverse Bennekel Culture: Bennekel is a cultural melting pot that reflects the great diversity of Eindhoven. Discover regional markets, real restaurants, and gathering places that honor this neighborhood's colorful fabric. Interact with locals, indulge in global cuisine, and feel the welcoming atmosphere of Bennekel.

Green Oasis in Vaartbroek: Vaartbroek astonishes with its verdant areas and serene atmosphere. Take a stroll in one of the neighborhood's parks, Henri Dunantpark, to experience some peace away from the bustle of the city. It's a secret haven where people and the environment live in harmony.

West Eindhoven: Embracing modern living while maintaining its traditions, Eindhoven West is a neighborhood changing. Explore cutting-edge cultural venues, fashionable eateries, and modern architecture. This canvas, which combines innovation and tradition, offers a look at Eindhoven as it changes over time.

Villapark's Cultural Treasures: Villapark is a residential community with a distinct cultural identity that is frequently disregarded. The Parktheater, which hosts a variety of shows and events, is located in this region. This hidden enclave has an artistic flavor thanks to local art shows and community meetings that you may find when strolling around the lanes adorned with trees.

Considerations for Exploration:

- Local Interaction: Talk to people in the area to learn about hidden treasures and local history. Local markets, small companies, and community activities frequently capture the true essence of an area.

- Transportation: Assess a neighborhood's suitability for walking or public transportation. While they might take some investigating, some lesser-known locations provide a more genuine experience.

- Timing: At certain periods, such as during cultural festivals or local gatherings, some communities might come to life. For a chance to witness the energy of these places, check the calendars in the area.

- Dining and Cafes: Take a look at some of the lesser-known districts' local restaurants and cafes. These undiscovered restaurants offer genuine flavors and a window into the way of life in the area.

In conclusion, there is much more to Eindhoven than only its well-known landmarks and well-liked neighborhoods. Savor the excitement of exploration as you meander through lesser-known areas and off-the-beaten-path sites. I hope your exploration of these lesser-known areas of Eindhoven reveals the unique and alluring spirit of the city and leaves you with unforgettable experiences. Cheers to your exploration!

Chapter 5

MUST-SEE SIGHTS

Iconic Landmarks in Eindhoven

Salutations, fellow travelers! The prominent sites that tell stories of the past and present are located in the center of Eindhoven, a city rich in invention and history. Let's go on an adventure to find the five sites that best represent Eindhoven and pique the interest of everyone who sees them.

Philips Stadion: Home of PSV Eindhoven

Location: 5616 NH Eindhoven, Frederiklaan 10a,

The Philips Stadion, home of PSV Eindhoven, is the tall structure that symbolizes the core of the city's football fanaticism. On game days, witness the electrifying atmosphere as supporters come together to support their favorite team. If you are unable to attend a game, guided tours offering an intimate glimpse into this iconic stadium are offered.

St. Catherine's Church: A Timeless Symbol

Location: 5611 GH Eindhoven, Kerkstraat 1.

Symbolizing Eindhoven's history for centuries, St. Catherine's Church dominates the skyline with its graceful spire. This Gothic church, which dates to the fifteenth century, welcomes you to enter and take in its imposing interior. The cathedral frequently holds cultural events that give its historic charm a modern twist.

The Blob: Modern Architecture in the Heart

Address: 18 Septemberplein, Eindhoven, 5611 AL

The Blob, a futuristic wonder that proudly stands at 18 Septemberplein, is a testament to Eindhoven's dedication to modern architecture. This striking building, which resembles a huge blob, holds offices and retail space. Observe how light plays off its glass façade throughout the day to create a dynamic visual display.

Van Abbemuseum: Where Art and Architecture Converge

Location: 5611 NH Eindhoven, Bilderdijklaan 10,

The Van Abbemuseum is an architectural marvel that seamlessly integrates into its surroundings, serving as more than just a museum. This museum, which was created by architect A.J. Kropholler, welcomes tourists to admire its avant-garde architecture in addition to housing an impressive collection of modern and contemporary art. View the fusion of architecture and art by exploring its varied displays.

De Admirant: Eindhoven's Glass Tower

Location: 5611 AZ Eindhoven, Emmasingel 3.

De Admirant is a glass tower that rises to a height of thirty meters and gives Eindhoven's skyline a contemporary feel. The city's dedication to creative urban design is demonstrated by this residential and commercial complex. Admire its reflective exterior and explore the vibrant neighborhood, which is home to stores, cafes, and cultural venues.

Museums and Art Galleries in Eindhoven

The rich cultural tapestry of Eindhoven is interwoven with themes of historical relevance and artistic expression. Discover the six museums and art galleries that entice art aficionados and inquisitive minds alike, providing an insightful tour of the city's artistic and intellectual landscapes.

1. Van Abbemuseum: Contemporary and Modern Art

Location: 5611 NH Eindhoven, Bilderdijklaan 10, Visit the Van Abbemuseum to explore the world of modern and contemporary art. Featuring pieces by well-known painters like Picasso and Mondrian, this museum encourages imagination and discussion. Accept the provocative displays that examine the relationship between art and society and challenge preconceived notions.

2. DAF Museum: Honoring Vehicle Innovation

Tongelresestraat 27, 5613 DA Eindhoven is the address. Inquire further at the DAF Museum, which honors the inventive spirit of the automotive sector in Eindhoven. Explore the development of DAF automobiles, from classic trucks to the newest innovations in technology. Discover the history of the city's automotive legacy by interacting with interactive displays and vintage models.

3. Eindhoven Museum: A Chronological Tour

Location: 5644 TV Eindhoven, Boutenslaan 161B
Explore the history of the city through an immersive experience at the Eindhoven Museum, where you may travel through time. Investigate historically accurate reconstructions, take in examples of traditional workmanship, and engage with interactive displays. This open-air museum provides a practical look into Eindhoven's past.

4. Design Academy Eindhoven: Showcasing Creative Innovation

Location: 5611 AZ Eindhoven, Emmasingel 14.
The Design Academy Eindhoven is a center for creative innovation located right in the middle of the city. It's not a standard museum, but its

presentations and exhibitions present innovative designs created by up-and-coming artists. Examine how design affects daily living and see how the future develops.

5. Museum door de Stad: Art in Public Spaces

Location: Various Eindhoven locations

The "Museum door de Stad," often known as "Museum by the City," is a creative idea that takes art to public spaces. Discover exhibits and public artworks strewn throughout the city as you explore Eindhoven. The boundaries between public areas and creative expression are blurred by this decentralized museum, which embraces the urban environment as its gallery.

6. Inkijkmuseum: A Peek into Artistic Expression

Location: Dommelstraat 2, 5611 CJ Eindhoven

The Inkijkmuseum, which translates to "Look-in Museum," extends an invitation for you to take a glimpse inside the realm of artistic creation. This little venue, which used to be a warehouse, accommodates a variety of performances, installations, and exhibitions. Accept the unexpected and lose yourself in this unusual haven of art's aura.

Architectural Marvels in Eindhoven

The skyline of Eindhoven is evidence of its dynamic architectural environment. Come explore six architectural wonders that demonstrate the city's dedication to urban development, creativity, and design.

Blobitecture Ingenuity: The Bulb

Address: 18 Septemberplein, Eindhoven, 5611 AL

The Blob is a cutting-edge architectural marvel that adorns 18 Septemberplein with its unique style. It is a modern emblem with its powerful structure and curved glass facade. In addition to being visually striking, this business and office space adds to the modern urban fabric of the metropolis.

Evoluon: A Futuristic Structure Resembling a UFO

Location: 5652 LA Eindhoven, Noord Brabantlaan 1A

See the futuristic charm of Evoluon, a skyscraper-like UFO that has come to represent Eindhoven. Evoluon, which was constructed in the 1960s, was first intended to be a museum of technology. Even though its purpose has changed, Eindhoven's dedication to invention is captivatingly reminded by its distinctive architecture.

Witte Dame: An Iconic Center of Design

Location: 5611 AZ Eindhoven, Emmasingel 14.

The Witte Dame, also known as the White Lady, is a stunning example of architecture that radiates class. It was once a Philips light bulb factory, but now it serves as a hub for design. The Witte Dame, with its white façade and Art Deco elements, is a brilliant representation of Eindhoven's inventiveness and design.

Vesteda Tower: Elegance of the Skyline

Vestdijk 29–31, 5611 CA Eindhoven is the address.

The elegant silhouette of the Vesteda Tower pierces the sky, making it a standout element of Eindhoven's cityscape. At ninety meters, this residential skyscraper provides a contemporary and opulent living environment.

Enjoy expansive city views from its upper levels while admiring Vestdijk's exquisite architecture.

Mariënhage: A Tasteful Fusion of the Past and the Present

Location: 5511 DH Eindhoven, Mariënburg 25,

The Augustinianum school, the monastery, and the Paterskerk are all part of the Mariënhage complex, which skillfully combines old and new architecture. The Paterskerk, in particular, gives this unusual combination a touch of timeless beauty with its magnificent stained glass windows and Gothic architecture.

Traverse: Eindhoven's Underground Marvel

Stationsplein 22, 5611 AC Eindhoven is the address.

Beneath the central station lies an underground passage called Traverse, which is a hidden architectural gem. Traverse is more than just a tunnel; it is intended to make pedestrian mobility easier. Its modern style, lit ceiling, and creative features offer an engrossing subterranean experience that highlights Eindhoven's dedication to avant-garde urban design.

Exploring Eindhoven's Architectural Landscape: Tips and Considerations

- Guided Tours: Take advantage of the guided tours that certain sites and museums provide. Knowledgeable guides offer perspectives on the background, design, and cultural importance of these recognizable buildings.
- Possibilities for Photography: The architectural marvels of Eindhoven provide fantastic photo ops. Capture the way light dances across contemporary façade, the grace of old structures, and the changing skyline of the metropolis.

- Participation in Events: See the schedules of events at architectural sites and museums. A few locations hold special occasions, shows, or open houses, offering one-of-a-kind chances to interact with Eindhoven's architectural legacy.
- Walking Routes: Plan your stroll to take in these sites and institutions at your own speed. Because of its compact design, Eindhoven is easy to explore on foot, letting you take in every architectural treasure.

I hope the city's dynamic fusion of innovation and history inspires you as we wrap up our tour of Eindhoven's famous buildings, museums, and architectural wonders. Discover the stories woven into the urban fabric of Eindhoven, whether you're drawn to the futuristic charm of Evoluon, the artistic manifestations within Van Abbemuseum, or the modern attraction of The Blob. I hope exploring these architectural and cultural treasures will enrich you as much as the city does. Cheers to your exploration!

Chapter 6

IMMERSE YOURSELF IN EINDHOVEN'S CULTURE

Local Festivals and Events in Eindhoven

Salutations, to friends who also enjoy colorful festivities and cross-cultural fun! The vibrant city of Eindhoven welcomes you to get lost in the variety of regional celebrations and activities. There are many different events in the city's calendar, ranging from traditional holidays to music and art exhibitions. Together, we will explore seven festivals and events that encapsulate the essence of Eindhoven that are not to be missed.

GLOW Eindhoven: A Dazzling Light Festival

Location: Throughout Eindhoven in different places.

Get ready to be mesmerized as GLOW Eindhoven turns the city into a canvas of light. Enthralling light installations, projections, and interactive displays are on display at this yearly light festival. Wander around famous avenues and sites like Catharinaplein and Stratumseind as the city comes to life with a kaleidoscope of hues. GLOW is a free event that happens every November and is a sight not to be missed by people of all ages.

King's Day: Orange-Hued Extravaganza

Location: Festivities taking place throughout the city

Come celebrate King's Day, the national celebration of the monarch's birthday, with the Dutch. Eindhoven bursts into a sea of orange, with canal excursions turning into floating parties and streets into vibrant marketplaces. Savor the festive atmosphere, street entertainment, and live music. Take part in the citywide celebrations on April 27th and wear your best orange attire to immerse yourself in the local culture.

Dutch Design Week: A Creative Showcase

Location: Several places, including Strijp-S

Those who are passionate about design, rejoice! Every year, Eindhoven hosts Dutch Design Week, an annual celebration of creativity and innovation. Investigate workshops, installations, and exhibitions covering a range of design specialties. The once-industrial Strijp-S district is transformed into a center for innovative design. Interact with up-and-coming artists, take in design projects, and learn about the direction that creativity is taking. Usually held in October, Dutch Design Week may need tickets for certain activities.

Carnaval Eindhoven: The Ultimate Dutch Celebration

Location: The market serves as the hub for citywide processions.

Discover Eindhoven's version of Carnaval, a vibrant and colorful event with parades, music, and revelry—the Dutch way. Come celebrate with the locals as they parade through the streets in extravagant costumes and revel in the joyous mood. The Markt, the main square, turns into the hub of the celebration. Carnaval is a distinctive and lively event that typically occurs in February.

Eindhoven Jazz Festival: Notes of Harmony

Location: Various jazz venues, including Muziekgebouw Eindhoven

Enjoy the pleasant atmosphere of the Eindhoven Jazz Festival, jazz enthusiasts. Take in a diverse mix of jazz concerts by regional and global performers. The city is alive with the passionate tones of this musical celebration, from opulent concert halls like Muziekgebouw Eindhoven to little jazz bars. The festival typically happens in May, and the cost of tickets varies based on the event and location.

FeelGood Market: Community, Creativity, and Cuisine

Location: Ketelhuisplein, Strijp-S

The FeelGood Market is a monthly event that unites a thriving community of artists, craftspeople, and master chefs. Visit vendors selling one-of-a-kind creations, original artwork, and a wide selection of foreign foods. Strijp-S's Ketelhuisplein became a center for artistic expression and cross-cultural dialogue. Savor the flavors of international food, interact with local artisans, and take in live music. Usually, the

FeelGood Market happens on the third Sunday of the month.

The Eindhoven Marathon: Race, Encourage, and Rejoice

Location: A marathon route that passes across several communities

Get your running shoes on or find a position along the course to support the runners at the Eindhoven Marathon. Every year, runners from all over the world come to this race, which highlights the city's beautiful neighborhoods and gorgeous scenery. Feel the pulse of the city whether you're a runner or a spectator at this exciting marathon, usually held in October. For information on registration and event details, see the official website.

Culinary Delights: Where and What to Eat

The food scene of Eindhoven offers a mouthwatering voyage through a variety of flavors, ranging from classic Dutch pastries to exotic international cuisine. Come with us as we explore seven culinary experiences that highlight the diverse and rich palette of the city.

Van Piere: A Literary Feast with Coffee

Location: 5611 AM Eindhoven, Nieuwe Emmasingel 48.

Start your day at Van Piere, a fun blend of café and bookshop. This literary refuge, which is centrally located, welcomes you to peruse its extensive book collection while enjoying a hot cup of coffee. In addition to serving a variety of pastries and light fare, the cafe creates the ideal atmosphere for both coffee and book lovers.

Usine: Industrial Chic Dining

Lichttoren 6, 5611 BJ Eindhoven is the address.

Nestled within the famous Lichttoren skyscraper, Usine flawlessly combines culinary brilliance with industrial elegance. The menu features a variety of regional and international cuisines that are presented artistically. Usine offers a gastronomic adventure in a setting that honors Eindhoven's industrial past, whether you choose a relaxed breakfast or an elegant evening.

Ketelhuis: Brunch in the Spirit of Creativity

Location: 5617 AE Eindhoven, Ketelhuisplein 1.

Experience the artistic atmosphere of Ketelhuis, situated in the bustling Strijp-S neighborhood. This once boiler house-turned-cultural hub has a varied brunch buffet to suit a range of palates. Savor a leisurely dinner in the vibrant Strijp-S ambiance, surrounded by live performances and contemporary art.

De Burger: West Eindhoven Gourmet Burgers

Willemstraat 29, 5611 HB Eindhoven is the address.

Visit De Burger in Eindhoven West to sample gourmet burgers. This small restaurant uses only the best ingredients to create delicious burgers. The menu offers something for every taste, from inventive vegetarian alternatives to traditional beef patties. For the perfect eating experience, pair your burger with crisp fries or a cool craft drink.

Saffraan: An Iranian Culinary Adventure

Location: 5611 KL Eindhoven, Grote Berg 38

Experience a gastronomic voyage to Iran at Saffraan, an Iranian eatery located in the center of Eindhoven. There is a delectable selection of Persian food on the menu, including creamy stews and fragrant kebabs. For those looking for a taste of Iran in Eindhoven, Saffraan stands out due to its genuine flavors and cozy, welcoming atmosphere.

Radio Royaal: Riverfront Dining by Industrial Chic

Ketelhuisplein 10, 5617 AE Eindhoven is the address.

Radio Royaal in Strijp-S provides an industrial-chic eating experience against the backdrop of the river. The restaurant, which blends contemporary food with vintage charm, was formerly a Philips radio plant. Savor a menu that emphasizes products that are locally sourced while taking in this architectural gem's distinctive atmosphere.

The Happiness Kitchen: Plant-Based Delights

Location: 5611 KH Eindhoven, Grote Berg 7.

At The Happiness Kitchen, a sanctuary for people looking for vegetarian and vegan options, indulge in plant-based delights.

This little restaurant, which is centrally located, specializes in creating dishes using fresh ingredients, in-season, and locally produced. For those who are concerned about their health, The Happiness Kitchen offers tasty wraps and filling bowls.

Tips for Culinary Exploration:

- Local Markets: For a taste of handmade goods, foreign cuisines, and unusual culinary discoveries, visit local markets like the FeelGood Market.
- Food Festivals: Stay informed about the events and food festivals that take place in Eindhoven. These events frequently highlight the gastronomic diversity of the city and provide a chance to sample a range of foods.
- Reservations: To guarantee a seat at a popular restaurant, particularly during

festivals and events, consider making reservations in advance.

- Culinary Tours: Embark on a culinary tour with knowledgeable locals to discover Eindhoven's top culinary destinations. These tours frequently offer insights into the history and culture of the city's cuisine.

Experience the unique cultural tapestry of Eindhoven through its festivals and delectable cuisine. Every encounter you have in Eindhoven adds a different brushstroke to the canvas of your vacation, whether you're dancing under the lights of GLOW or enjoying the flavors of Iranian food at Saffraan. So, my dear travelers, enjoy the celebrations and the delectable food that this vibrant Dutch city has to offer. Salutations and bon appétit to times to remember!

Nightlife and Entertainment in Eindhoven

Eindhoven is transformed into a colorful world of pulsating sounds, unique places, and unforgettable encounters when the sun sets over its bustling streets. Take a trip with me through the entertainment and nightlife of Eindhoven, where the city comes to life after dark.

1. Stratumseind: The Pulsating Center of Nightlife in Eindhoven

Location: 5611 EP Eindhoven, Stratumseind

Get ready to experience the vibrant energy of Stratumseind, the famous nightlife zone of Eindhoven. With its wide selection of pubs, clubs, and entertainment establishments, this busy boulevard is a center of activity. Stratumseind provides a varied nightlife experience, ranging from hip nightclubs with world-class DJs to warm pubs where locals congregate. Everyone may find something they enjoy on this lively street, whether they prefer live music or electronic rhythms.

2. Effenaar: A Strijp-S Musical Paradise

Dommelstraat 2, 5611 CK Eindhoven is the address.

Effenaar in Strijp-S is a must-visit for music lovers looking for a vibrant venue. A varied array of live performances spanning genres from rock and pop to techno and indie takes place at this legendary music arena. For information on festivals, club nights, and concerts, see the event calendar. Modern sound equipment and an industrial-chic atmosphere make Effenaar a top choice for exceptional musical experiences.

3. Kazerne: A Combination of Design, Art, and Nightlife

Address: 2-8 Paradijslaan, 5611 KN Eindhoven

Enter the enthralling realm of Kazerne, where nightlife, design, and the arts all coexist harmoniously. This versatile space serves as both a bar and a gallery, offering a classy environment for discovering different cultures. Savor a carefully chosen assortment of handcrafted drinks and cocktails while taking in the artistic energy all around you. Kazerne creates an unforgettable atmosphere with her distinctive fusion of entertainment and elegance.

4. Café Thomas: Craft Beer and a Cozy Getaway

Address: 32 Stratumseind, 5611 Eindhoven ET.

Situated in the center of Stratumseind, Café Thomas provides a comfortable haven for individuals looking for a lively yet relaxed ambiance. Beer lovers will find this pub, which is well-known for its wide assortment of craft brews, to be a sanctuary. Enjoy the spirit of Eindhoven's social life at Café Thomas, where you may relax on the terrace or strike up a spirited conversation at the bar.

5. Area51 Skatepark: Beyond Skating Under the Stars

Location: 5617 AB Eindhoven, Klokgebouw 51

At the famous Klokgebouw, Area 51 Skatepark offers a distinctive nightlife experience. This unique location doubles as a vibrant venue for festivals, concerts, and cultural gatherings in addition to being a skatepark. For live acts, DJ sets, and themed parties, check the schedule. Area51 Skatepark is a unique place to go on an evening adventure, whether you enjoy skating or just take in a unique atmosphere.

6. De Vooruitgang: Chic Eating and Mood Lighting

Markt 11, 5611 EB Eindhoven is the address.

Start your evening at De Vooruitgang with dinner and move smoothly into the late hours of the night. This chic location mixes a chic restaurant with a lively bar scene in the center of the city on Markt Square. Enjoy a wide selection of international dishes, and as the evening wears on, take in the venue's transition into a vibrant social hub for drinks.

7. Fifth NRE: A Nightlife and Culture Fusion

Location: 5513 CM Eindhoven, Nachtegaallaan 15.

Located in a former energy business building, Fifth NRE is a symbol of the merging of nightlife and culture. This multipurpose venue holds a variety of events, including art exhibitions, cultural meetings, DJ sets, and live performances. The venue's personality, combined with its creative atmosphere and industrial setting, invites you to investigate the nexus between entertainment and creativity.

Tips for a Memorable Night Out in Eindhoven:

- Examine Event Calendars: To find out about upcoming live events and themed parties, examine the event calendars of places like Effenaar and Area51 Skatepark before leaving.

- Discover Stratumseind: Stroll around Stratumseind to find hidden gems, ranging from fun bars to vibrant nightclubs. With a variety of options to suit every taste, the street comes to life.

- Late-Night Bites: If you're looking for something to eat late at night, consider restaurants like De Vooruitgang, where you can eat and then easily stroll around and take in the evening atmosphere.

- Make Plans for Unique Events: Especially during festivals and cultural festivities, keep an eye out for themed nights and unique events. The nightlife of Eindhoven frequently features unusual and unforgettable events.

- Public Transportation: Arrange your transportation ahead of time, particularly if you're visiting several locations. The public transportation alternatives in Eindhoven facilitate safe and convenient city mobility.

The city's nightlife entices you to join in the celebration as the stars light up the Eindhoven sky. Eindhoven's nighttime scenery guarantees an amazing experience, whether you're drinking specialty drinks at Kazerne, dancing to rhythms in Stratumseind, or taking in live music at Effenaar. So, my dear night owls, welcome the enthusiasm, check out the venues, and let Eindhoven's beat lead you to an exciting and entertaining evening. To a lively evening spent in the center of the Netherlands!

Chapter 7

OUTDOOR ADVENTURES

Parks and Green Spaces in Eindhoven

Welcome to Eindhoven's green side, where the city's luxuriant natural areas coexist peacefully with urban living. Let me, as your friendly guide, show you around the parks and green areas that provide a cool escape from the bustle of the city.

Stadswandelpark: A Calm Urban Sanctuary

Location: 5615 EB Eindhoven, Alberdingk Thijmlaan

Located in the center of Eindhoven, Stadswandelpark, often known as City Walk Park, is a calm haven. This large park features colorful flower beds, calm lakes, and meandering trails. Stadswandelpark is a great place for a peaceful picnic or a stroll. Its aesthetic appeal is enhanced by the sculptures and artworks that are there.

Year-round, the park offers both locals and tourists a lovely getaway.

Genneper Parken: Environment and Pleasure

Location: 5644 RX Eindhoven, Antoon Coolenlaan 1.

Genneper Parken is a vast green space that blends leisure activities and the natural world. Discover the charming paths for strolling, bask in the splendor of Genneper Watermills, or experience a taste of country life by stopping by the Genneper Hoeve farm. A round of golf, swimming at the Tongelreep pool, or canoeing are available for sports enthusiasts. Genneper Parken offers nature enthusiasts and energetic people a vibrant blend of vegetation and a variety of activities.

Eindhoven Garden's Parktheater: A Cultural Haven

Elzentlaan 50, 5615 CN Eindhoven is the address.

The Parktheater Garden, a secret gem where culture and nature collide, is tucked away within the grounds of Parktheater Eindhoven. Encircled by sculptures and trees, this enchanted green area offers a peaceful atmosphere for reflection. When the garden becomes an intimate cultural space, take a stroll, observe the creative components, and maybe catch an outdoor concert or event.

Henri Dunantpark: A Congenial Getaway

Location: 5623 LJ Eindhoven, Dunantweg

Henri Dunantpark is a family-friendly hideaway with a range of recreational attractions, named after the Red Cross founder. Play a round of mini-golf with the kids, take them to explore the playgrounds, or have a picnic by the pond. The park is a welcoming location for a laid-back day out with loved ones because of its well-kept grass and shady places.

Gender Park: The Harmony of Nature and Art

Location: 5616 Eindhoven, Genderpark

Gender Park is a peaceful haven where art and nature coexist peacefully. There are bike and walking trails in this park, so visitors may explore its verdant spaces and come across art exhibits as they go. For those looking to connect with nature and the arts, Gender Park offers a serene haven with its serene environment and picturesque surroundings.

Recreational Activities: Outdoor Active Sports in Eindhoven

For those looking for adventure and energetic hobbies, Eindhoven's thriving outdoor scene provides a wide range of recreational opportunities. Let's explore the range of choices that appeal to those seeking a more relaxed outdoor experience as well as thrill-seekers.

Cycling in Eindhoven: Take Two Wheels to See the City

With a vast network of bike paths and bike lanes, Eindhoven is a cyclist's dream come true. Take a bike rental from one of the city's many stores and go around Eindhoven at your speed. Riding a bicycle is an excellent way to experience both the natural and urban environments, whether you decide to peddle through parks, along picturesque canals, or through the city center.

Strijp-S: Urban Exploration and Creativity

Location: 5617 Eindhoven, Strijp-S

Described as an urban playground for creativity and adventure, Strijp-S is more than just a district. Explore the street art-adorned industrial-chic streets, stop by concept stores, and take in the lively vibe. Additionally, Strijp-S holds festivals, markets, and events that highlight the vibrant energy of Eindhoven's creative scene. If any special events coincide with your stay, check the events calendar.

High Tech Campus Eindhoven: Innovation and Nature

High Tech Campus, 5656 AE Eindhoven is the address.

The High Tech Campus is a verdant haven where technology and the natural world coexist, offering more than just innovative opportunities. The campus offers a unique combination of state-of-the-art technology and natural surroundings with its walking and cycling routes. Enjoy a stroll around the campus, check out the creative architecture, and maybe you'll happen upon one of the occasionally happening outdoor events or exhibitions that adorn this vibrant area.

Tongelreep Swimming Pool: Water-Based Experiences

Location: 5644 RX Eindhoven, Antoon Coolenlaan 1.

Explore underwater experiences at the Tongelreep Swimming Centre. This brand-new facility has recreational spaces and an Olympic-sized pool among its many pools. Tongelreep offers a revitalizing respite for anyone looking to unwind by the pool, whether they are avid swimmers, a family looking for water fun, or someone else entirely. For information about swimming instruction, water aerobics, and special events, see the schedule.

City Golf Eindhoven: Tee Off in the Heart of the City

Location: Various spots throughout the city, such as Stadswandelpark.

Try City Golf Eindhoven for a distinctive take on the traditional sport. Set out on a golfing journey across urban landscapes from a variety of city locations, such as Stadswandelpark. This nontraditional game of golf blends the excitement of making the ideal shot with sightseeing. City Golf Eindhoven provides a distinctive and enjoyable experience for all golfers, experienced or not.

Day Trips and Nature Excursion

Due to its advantageous location, Eindhoven is close to many picturesque locations and natural treasures. Come along on a virtual tour of day outings and outdoor adventures that showcase the breathtaking scenery that surrounds the city.

De Groote Heide: A Natural Border

Location: Strabrechtseheideweg 31, 5591 TN Heeze.

De Groote Heide, often known as The Great Heath, is a wide natural border that is only a short drive from Eindhoven. This vast heathland provides beautiful paths for bicycling and strolling, letting you enjoy the peace of the natural world. Wander through the tranquil Strabrechtse Heide, renowned for its vivid purple heather blossoms in late summer, and take in the clean, fresh air.

The Van Gogh-Roosegaarde Cycle: Combining Art and Nature

Location: 5691 EN, N615, En Breugel

Take a day trip to the Van Gogh-Roosegaarde Cycle Path and combine art and nature. This unusual route, which is close to Eindhoven, is lit up at night by entrancing patterns that are reminiscent of Vincent van Gogh's Starry Night. Take a bike rental, ride the illuminated route, and witness the fascinating convergence of technology, art, and environment.

Oisterwijkse Bossen en Vennen: Woodlands and Ponds

Location: 5062 SK, Oisterwijk Oisterwijk

Explore the Oisterwijkse Bossen en Vennen, a picturesque area featuring ponds and forests. Nestled amidst beautiful vegetation, this natural reserve is just a short drive from Eindhoven and offers a network of walking and cycling trails. Discover the ponds that are crystal clear, stroll about the picturesque surroundings, and take in the variety of plants and animals that call this natural sanctuary home.

Klimrijk Brabant: An Adventure in the Treetops

Klaterlaan 1, 5688 GP Oirschot is the location.

Visit Klimrijk Brabant for an action-packed and scenic day. This hard obstacle course is hanging among the trees at this treetop adventure park, which is located close to Eindhoven. Sail through ziplines, put your agility to the test, and take in the expansive treetop views.

Offering a variety of courses for varying ability levels, Klimrijk Brabant is a thrilling day trip destination for adventure seekers.

Nationaal Park De Loonse en Drunense Duinen: Sand Dunes Serenity

Location: Roestelbergseweg 2, 5171 RL Kaatsheuvel, Visitor Center Roestelberg

Take a picturesque trip to Nationaal Park De Loonse en Drunense Duinen, a place renowned for its enormous sand dunes and mesmerizing scenery. Just a short drive from Eindhoven, this national park features hiking and cycling paths among pine forests and shifting dunes. Savor the tranquility of this exceptional natural treasure while exploring the varied terrain and capturing breathtaking views from the higher dunes.

Exploring Eindhoven's Outdoor Wonders: Tips and Considerations

Transportation: For day trips, schedule your transportation in advance. Make sure your travel to and from the outdoor excursions goes smoothly, whether you want to use public transportation, guided tours, or a rental car.

- Weather Awareness: Before engaging in any outdoor activity, check the weather forecast. Particularly for outdoor activities where the weather may affect your enjoyment, dress appropriately.
- Equipment Rental: Check with nearby stores regarding renting equipment for sports like cycling. Bike rentals are widely available in Eindhoven, so you can make sure you have the equipment you need to explore the city and its environs.
- Nature Reserves: Adhere to the regulations governing parks and nature reserves. Watch

out for trails that are designated, abide by environmental regulations, and enjoy the beauty of nature while causing the least amount of ecological disturbance.

Parks, leisure pursuits, and neighboring natural beauties in Eindhoven encourage you to embrace nature in a variety of ways. Every activity, whether it's relaxing at Stadswandelpark, riding about the city, or taking a day trip to De Groote Heide, reveals a different aspect of Eindhoven's verdant appeal. So, my fellow nature lovers, get ready for an exciting journey to the center of the Netherlands, where modern living coexists peacefully with the natural world. Cheers to your exploration!

Chapter 8

THRILLING
EXPERIENCES

Adrenaline-Pumping Activities in Eindhoven

Salutations, adventure seekers! Eindhoven is a playground for thrill-seekers as well as a metropolis of technology and design. Come along on an exciting tour through the adrenaline-pumping adventures available in and around Eindhoven.

Indoor Skydiving at City Skydive Eindhoven:

Address: 3400 Flight Forum, 5657 EW Eindhoven At City Skydive Eindhoven, experience the exhilaration of freefall without really jumping out of an airplane. This indoor skydiving facility allows you to feel like you're flying through a vertical wind tunnel. Whether you've skydived before or not, the knowledgeable instructors at City Skydive guarantee a thrilling and safe experience. The institution provides a range of options, such as advanced training and introductory courses. For information about reservations and operating hours, see their website.

Karting at De Landsard: Race to Victory!

Location: 5657 EA Eindhoven, Landsard 4, Landsard Beach

At the exhilarating outdoor karting circuit De Landsard, which is situated on the sands of Landsard Beach, you may unleash your inner racer. Enjoy the breeze in your hair as you make your way over difficult curves and straightaways. For both individuals and groups, De Landsard offers an exhilarating experience in karting, regardless of skill level. For more on price, special events, and track availability, see their website.

Climbing at Monk Bouldergym Eindhoven:

The address is 500 Kastanjelaan, 5616 LZ Eindhoven.

Climbers are invited to Monk Bouldergym Eindhoven to overcome walls with different levels of difficulty. Without the use of ropes, bouldering enables climbers to concentrate on their strength and technique. For climbers of all abilities, from novices to experts, the gym offers a dynamic environment. Every time you visit Monk Bouldergym, you can expect a novel and demanding experience because the routes are constantly reset. For information on membership options, day passes, and operating hours, visit their website.

Wakeboarding at Burnside Cablepark:

Location: 5684 NP Best, Veenplasweg 5

Burnside Cablepark is the place to go if you're looking for aquatic thrills. Feel the exhilaration of wakeboarding while being hauled across the water via a cable system. Burnside features a lake with obstacles, ramps, and jumps for an exhilarating ride for both novice and expert riders. Water sports fans can access the park by renting equipment from it. For information on reservations, pricing, and operating hours, see their website.

Unique Experiences for Adventure Seekers

Beyond the norm, Eindhoven provides one-of-a-kind encounters that satisfy the traveler's soul. Let's explore some unusual pursuits that are sure to make you remember them forever.

Escape Room Strijp-S: Unleash Your Inner Detective

Location: 5617 AC Eindhoven, Klokgebouw 225

Take on an exhilarating task at Escape Room Strijp-S, situated within the renowned Klokgebouw. Get your group together and enter a mysterious and puzzle-filled realm. Break codes, solve riddles, and piece together the plot within the allotted time. With several themed chambers, such as the fascinating "Mindcrime" and "The Raadsel van de Klok," Escape Room Strijp-S offers thrill-seekers of all ages an unforgettable trip. To schedule your escape excursion and view their opening hours, go to their website.

Virtual Reality at Enversed VR Center

Location: 5617 BC Eindhoven, Torenallee 20

Explore the world of virtual reality by visiting the Enversed VR Center. This state-of-the-art venue provides a range of virtual reality experiences, including exhilarating games and realistic simulations. Put on your virtual reality headset and go on experiences that challenge reality, whether it's facing off against virtual enemies or exploring far-off realms. Both individuals and groups can have an engaging and enjoyable retreat at Enversed VR Center. For information on reservations and available experiences, see their website.

Zombie Apocalypse Experience at Area 51

Location: 5617 AB Eindhoven, Klokgebouw 51

At Area 51, be ready for a singular and terrifying experience. In the Zombie Apocalypse Experience, visitors are thrust into a zombie-infested post-apocalyptic world. Test your survival skills while navigating through realistic environments with authentic weaponry. For those seeking a thrilling encounter with a cinematic twist, this heart-pounding adventure is perfect. For more on the event, bookings, and possible dates, visit the Area 51 website.

Flyboarden at AquaBest: Soar Above the Water

Address: Aquabest Recreation Plas, Ekkersweijer 1, 5681 RZ Best

Discover what it's like to soar above the water with Flyboarden at AquaBest. Put on a flyboard and learn how to hover and execute airborne feats. Flyboards use water jets to push users into the air. Flyboarding is a unique and exhilarating water experience that AquaBest offers to both rookie and expert flyboarders. For information on reservations, pricing, and availability, see their website.

Extreme Sports in and Around Eindhoven

Extreme sports aficionados can find their heaven in Eindhoven and its environs if they're looking for the ultimate burst of adrenaline. Prepare to push yourself to the limit with these intense exercises.

Paragliding at Ginkelse Heide:

Location: About 45 minutes from Eindhoven, near Ginkelse Heide in Ede.

Paragliding over Ginkelse Heide's scenic scenery will allow you to soar like a bird. Sail through the sky and enjoy the freedom of flight while soaking in expansive vistas of the surrounding landscape. Tandem flights are provided by several paragliding schools in the area, making this thrilling experience accessible to both novices and thrill-seekers. For information on booking, cost, and availability, get in touch with the nearby paragliding schools.

Skydiving at Skydive ENPC

Location: Luchthavenweg 25, 5657 EA Eindhoven, Eindhoven Airport.

Skydive ENPC, conveniently located near Eindhoven Airport, offers tandem skydiving experiences. Take the ultimate leap. You will experience the exhilaration of terminal velocity as you freefall thousands of feet while strapped to an expert instructor. Afterward, the parachute will deploy, allowing for a smooth glide back to Earth. Enjoy breathtaking vistas of the Eindhoven area while you set off on this exhilarating journey. For information on jump options, rates, and bookings, see the Skydive ENPC website.

Off-Roading at Experience Island: Conquer the Terrain

Location: 30 minutes or so from Eindhoven at Veerplas 4, 5172 NP Kaatsheuvel.

At Experience Island, you may unleash your inner off-road enthusiast and conquer the challenging terrain at your leisure. Get on an ATV or a quad bike and go through difficult courses that will put your driving prowess to the test. In a controlled and safe environment, feel the rush of overcoming hurdles, mud pits, and uneven terrain. For information about off-roading packages, availability, and reservation details, visit Experience Island's website.

Caving at Adventure Mine Valkenburg

Address: 31 Daalhemerweg, 6301 BJ Van der Geul, Valkenburg (about 1.5 hours from Eindhoven).

Experience the underground world of Adventure Mine Valkenburg by going caving. Discover the mysteries that lie beneath the surface of the planet by exploring enigmatic caves, tunnels, and chambers. Through this underground realm, participants crawl, climb, and navigate under the guidance of knowledgeable guides. For those looking for a unique underground adventure, Adventure Mine Valkenburg offers an exciting caving experience. For information about reservations, prices, and available tours, see their website.

Safety Tips for Extreme Adventures

- Professional Advice: Only take part in extreme sports under the supervision of qualified experts. Observe the safety precautions and advice that instructors or adventure facilities provide.
- Equipment Inspection: Verify that every piece of gear utilized for extreme sports is in good working order. Observe the facility's

and the instructors' safety instructions and inspections.

- Physical Preparation: Before partaking in strenuous activities, evaluate your level of physical fitness and any underlying medical issues. Certain excursions could call for particular physical preparation.
- Weather Considerations: Pay attention to the weather, particularly if you're going outside. Weather conditions can affect extreme sports, so plan and check the forecast.
- Attend the health and safety informational sessions that adventure facilities offer. Recognize emergency protocols and rules in case of unanticipated events.

Experiences that will make your heart race, extreme sports options, and unusual activities in Eindhoven appeal to thrill-seekers of all stripes. Every adventure, whether it's conquering off-road obstacles at Experience Island, defying gravity at City Skydive, or solving escape room secrets in Strijp-S, guarantees incredible adrenaline.

Therefore, daring adventurers, buckle in, embrace the rush, and let Eindhoven's adventurous side take you into an exciting new world!

Chapter 9

PRACTICAL INFORMATION

Safety and Emergency Information

Welcome to Eindhoven, where we take your safety and well-being very seriously. I'll act as your guide and provide you with all the information you need to make sure you have a safe and pleasurable visit.

Contacts for Emergencies: Dial 112, the universal emergency number, in the event of any emergency. This puts you in contact with emergency responders such as the police, fire, and ambulance services. If you need assistance that is not urgent, call the local police at 0900-8844.

Medical Support: If you need medical care, Eindhoven has top-notch hospitals. A premier medical facility is the Catharina Hospital, located at Michelangelolaan 2, 5623 EJ Eindhoven. In case of an emergency, the emergency room is available around the clock.

Travel Guard: Think about getting comprehensive travel insurance before your trip. This guarantees coverage for unanticipated events such as travel cancellations and unexpected medical costs. For more information about coverage and emergency assistance, contact your insurance company.

Individual Security: Though common sense safety precautions are advised, Eindhoven is generally a safe city. Be mindful of your possessions, particularly in busy places, and watch out for pickpockets. When taking public transportation at night, stay in well-lit places and pay attention to your surroundings.

Currency and Payment

Comprehending the currency and modes of payment guarantees seamless transactions throughout your visit to Eindhoven. Now let's discuss the fundamentals of money.

Like the Netherlands, Eindhoven uses the Euro (EUR) as its official currency. Make sure you have enough euros on hand for any last-minute purchases, local markets, or locations that might not take credit or debit cards.

In Eindhoven, ATMs and currency exchange ATMs are extensively distributed and let you take out euros using a debit or credit card. Major banks also provide currency exchange services; one such bank is ING Bank, located at Hooghuisstraat 1, 5611 GS Eindhoven.

Debit and Credit Cards In Eindhoven, credit and debit cards are commonly accepted, particularly in stores, eateries, and lodging facilities. Visa and Mastercard are widely accepted, while acceptance of American Express and Diners Club may be more restricted. To prevent any problems with card transactions, let your bank know when you will be traveling.

Payments via Contactless In Eindhoven, contactless payment systems are accepted. Contactless cards and mobile payments are widely accepted by businesses, offering a practical and hygienic method of completing transactions.

Tipping Culture: Tipping is customary in the Netherlands but not required. It is traditional in restaurants to leave a little tip if service is not included, or to round up the bill. Small tips are also appreciated by service personnel and taxi drivers.

Communication Tips

Effective communication makes your stay in Eindhoven more enjoyable. Let's look at some advice for ensuring smooth encounters and relationships while you're visiting.

Official Language: Dutch is the official language in Eindhoven. Even while many people in the region speak English, particularly at tourist destinations and businesses, picking up a few simple Dutch phrases can be a fun way to strike up a conversation with locals.

Language Assistance: Tourist information offices, like the one at Stationsplein 17, 5611 AC Eindhoven, provide helpful information in many languages and linguistic aid in case you run into problems communicating.

Public Transport: The public transit system in Eindhoven is effective, and signs and announcements are frequently posted in both Dutch and English. Since most transport employees know English, getting help when needed is simple.

Wi-Fi accessibility: Use the free Wi-Fi that is offered in many cafes, hotels, and public areas to stay connected. You can get a local SIM card from mobile service providers like Vodafone or KPN if you need one.

Sensitivity to Culture: Eindhoven values cultural awareness and welcomes a diverse community. To promote constructive relationships, respect regional traditions, and keep cultural differences in mind.

Centers for Tourist Information: For information, maps, and brochures, visit tourist information centers. The Eindhoven Visitor Center, located at Stationsplein 17, 5611 AC Eindhoven, has a convenient location and friendly staff.

In summary, you will be greeted warmly in Eindhoven, and these tips will help you go around the city with assurance. Enjoying the rich culture, relishing in local food, or discovering its technological marvels all count toward a memorable trip, but what really matters are your financial transactions, communication encounters, and safety. I hope your stay in Eindhoven is full of happiness, learning, and deep relationships!

Chapter 10

Sustainable Travel in Eindhoven

Eco-Friendly Initiatives in Eindhoven

Welcome to Eindhoven, a city whose dedication to environmental responsibility and sustainable living is deeply ingrained in its culture. As your tour guide, I'm thrilled to present the different programs that help Eindhoven get closer to a more environmentally friendly future.

Parks and Green Areas: There are lots of parks and green areas in Eindhoven, which act as the city's "lungs." One of the best examples is Stadswandelpark, which is situated at Alberdingk Thijmlaan, 5615 EB Eindhoven. This large park serves as a peaceful haven and supports the ecological equilibrium of the city. Year-round, it's a great place for a picnic in the middle of the forest or a stroll.

Cycling Culture for a Sustainable Commute: Accept the bicycle culture of Eindhoven as an eco-friendly, low-emission form of transportation. Take a ride on one of the many rental bikes available in the city and discover its environmentally friendly infrastructure. The city's support of cycling is not just practical; it also reflects its commitment to reducing the environmental impact of transportation.

Green Architecture: Changing Cityscape Observe how green architecture projects are changing Eindhoven's cityscape. A good example is the Mariënhage complex, which is situated at Augustijnendreef 15, 5611 CS Eindhoven. A harmonious urban environment is created by combining modern sustainable design with historic buildings. Discover the area, take in the harmonious blend of architecture, and recognize the ways that Eindhoven integrates green design into its growth.

Sustainable Shopping at Strijp-S: Visit Strijp-S, a cutting-edge neighborhood located at 5617 Eindhoven where sustainability is prioritized. Investigate concept stores, galleries, and boutiques that support locally produced and environmentally responsible goods. Strijp-S is more than simply a place to shop; it's evidence of Eindhoven's dedication to assisting companies that value environmentally friendly operations.

Community Gardens: Creating Green Spaces with Community Gardens Visit the community gardens in Eindhoven, like the one in Karel Vermeerenplantsoen, 5622 CC Eindhoven, and get involved. These areas support sustainable activities like urban gardening while strengthening ties within the community. Discover how Eindhoven encourages its citizens to contribute to creating green spaces by exploring the garden and interacting with the inhabitants.

Responsible Tourism Practices

Responsible tourism in Eindhoven is a way of life that balances environmental awareness with cultural experience. It is not just a notion. Let's explore the behaviors that this vibrant city defines as responsible tourism.

Observance of regional customs and culture: Become fully immersed in the culture of the place by honoring traditions and customs. Respect the artwork and follow museum protocol when visiting locations such as the Van Abbemuseum, located at Bilderdijklaan 10, 5611 NH Eindhoven. Respecting and understanding the local way of life improves your experience and encourages constructive relationships.

Encouraging Small Companies: The Heart of Eindhoven Boosts the local economy by lending a hand to independent companies. Discover the varied selections found in neighborhood stores, markets, and restaurants, such as those in the Strijp-S neighborhood, and savor goods that showcase the inventiveness and spirit of entrepreneurship of the city. Your purchases encourage sustainable economic practices in addition to helping the neighborhood.

Reduction of Waste and Recycling Initiatives: Eindhoven aggressively encourages recycling and waste minimization. Use the proper recycling containers located throughout the city to help with these efforts. Reusable products are frequently encouraged at cafés and restaurants, so take advantage of this by using a reusable water bottle and, when possible, choosing eco-friendly packaging.

Mindful Consumption: Food and Dining: Discover restaurants that prioritize using sustainable and locally sourced ingredients to enjoy dining responsibly. The Ketelhuis in Ketelhuisplein 1, 5617 AE Eindhoven, is a great example. This popular restaurant promotes sustainability in its food selections while still providing a great eating experience.

Environmental Awareness in Events: Participate in environmental awareness-promoting events. Numerous eco-friendly events take place in Eindhoven, like the FeelGood Market, which is frequently held at Strijp-S. This market reduces the environmental impact of consumerism while promoting a sense of community by showcasing sustainable, locally produced goods.

Cultural Sensitivity and Responsible Travel

Local Customs: To ensure polite interactions with the community, familiarize oneself with customs and norms specific to the area. This entails knowing how to meet people, be polite, and act appropriately in public areas.

Nature Reserves: Follow established trails and rules when exploring parks or nature reserves. Honor the plants and animals, and do not interfere with the ecosystem.

Cultural Events: Respect regional norms and traditions when taking part in festivals or other cultural events. Respect people's right to privacy and, if necessary, obtain consent before taking any pictures.

Public Areas: Keep these areas tidy by placing trash in the appropriate containers. When not in use, turn off lights and electronics to conserve resources.

Supporting Local Arts: Get involved in your community's arts scene by going to shows, exhibits, and other activities. Preserving cultural history is aided by the support of regional artists and creatives.

Because of its dedication to eco-friendly projects and ethical tourism, Eindhoven encourages travelers to explore with an awareness of their cultural and environmental responsibilities. Through adopting eco-friendly behaviors, honoring regional traditions, and backing neighborhood projects, you'll not only have a rewarding vacation but also help preserve Eindhoven's distinct charm. I hope your trip to Eindhoven brings you both environmental tranquility and cultural enrichment! Safe travels!

CONCLUSION

Highlights of Eindhoven Revealed

As we come to the end of our tour of Eindhoven, let's pause to review the colorful mosaic of marvels that characterize this thriving metropolis. Modern technology, creative marvels, eco-friendly projects, and delectable food are all interwoven in a story that captivates the senses and inspires a spirit of adventure in Eindhoven.

- **Technological Wonders:** Unveiling Innovations Reputable establishments like the High Tech Campus and the Eindhoven University of Technology demonstrate Eindhoven's technological ability. The city is a center for technological breakthroughs and discoveries because of its dedication to innovation and research, which fosters a dynamic environment.

- **Art and Design:** Unrestricted Creativity Immerse yourself in the world of design and art at Strijp-S and the Van Abbemuseum. The city of Eindhoven is known for its dynamic galleries, exhibitions, and urban spaces. Its creative spirit knows no bounds.

- **Green Oases:** The Warm Hug of Nature explores the peace of Eindhoven's green areas, which include the large Stadswandelpark and community gardens. The city's commitment to sustainability and eco-friendly practices is evident in its bike culture, green architecture, and verdant environs, which encourage both locals and visitors to get outside and enjoy nature.

- **Gourmet Treats:** A Taste Explosion The culinary scene of Eindhoven is a celebration of regional products and a wide range of flavors. Savor delicious meals at eateries such as the Ketelhuis and visit the FeelGood Market to sample the sustainably produced, locally sourced fare.

- **Exciting Activities:** Experiences Unlocked Eindhoven has a plethora of heart-pounding activities, unusual encounters, and extreme sports to offer the thrill-seeker. The city's daring side offers excitement at every step, whether you're mastering off-road obstacles at Experience Island or defying gravity at City Skydive.

- **Participation in the Community:** Building Relationships Participate in local markets, events, and cultural activities to foster community engagement. Due to Eindhoven's dedication to responsible tourism, travelers are encouraged to embrace cultural sensitivity, patronize neighborhood businesses, and take part in environmentally friendly events.

Best Wishes for Travel and Farewell: Until We Meet Again

As our time in Eindhoven draws to a conclusion, please accept my sincere goodbye and best wishes for your future adventures. May you always be struck by the technological wonders, creative genius, and breathtaking scenery of Eindhoven.

May your experiences be treasured, whether you take away a fragment of Eindhoven's inventiveness, a stroke of its imagination, or the peace of its green areas.

Take the spirit of Eindhoven with you on your travels; it is a city that never stops changing, where tradition and innovation coexist, and where there is always a tale to be told around every corner. May your travels be full of happiness, exploration, and the comfort of treasured memories till we cross paths again.

I hope your journey is as exciting and full of adventure as the one Eindhoven has so kindly shared with us. Safe travels, my explorer. Goodbye, and may the journey ahead bring with it unending opportunities and new perspectives.

APPENDIX

Useful Contacts in Eindhoven

Having useful contacts makes traveling to Eindhoven easier and more pleasurable. The following connections are vital to have on hand:

Services for Emergencies:

- Emergency Number: 112 for Fire, Police, and Ambulance
- Police Assistance That Is Not Urgent: 0900-8844

Health Services:

- The emergency department at Catharina Hospital: Michelangelolaan 2, 5623 EJ Eindhoven is the address. Get in touch with Catharina Hospital

Information for Travelers:

- Visitors Center in Eindhoven: Stationsplein 17, 5611 AC Eindhoven is the address. Contact: Visitor Center Eindhoven

Transport:

- Information on Public Transportation: Get in touch with 9292 Trip Planner

Services for Taxis:

- Make contact with ride-sharing applications or local taxi services.

Services for Lost and Found:

- Make contact with the local government or the places where missing goods were found.

Useful Phrases

Even though most people in Eindhoven speak English, knowing a few words in Dutch is appreciated. The following are some helpful phrases to improve your communication:

- Hello: Hallo
- Thank you: Dank je wel (informal), Dank u wel (formal)
- Goodbye: Tot ziens
- Excuse me/Pardon: Pardon
- Please: Alsjeblieft (informal), Alstublieft (formal)
- Yes/No: Ja/Nee

- Do you speak English?: Spreekt u Engels?
- Where is...?: Waar is...?
- How much is this?: Hoeveel kost dit?
- Help!: Hulp!

Glossary of Local Terms

Learn some local lingo to make your way about Eindhoven like a travel pro:

Strijp-S: A cutting-edge neighborhood renowned for its eco-friendly projects and creative spaces.

Ketelhuis: A popular cultural destination that offers sustainably focused food options.

Stadswandelpark: A vast park offering a calm haven in the middle of the city.

FeelGood Market: Diverse marketplace featuring regional, eco-friendly goods and delicious food.

High Tech Campus: Eindhoven's preeminent center for innovation and technology.

Catharina Hospital: A reputable healthcare center providing a variety of services.

Van Abbemuseum: Well-known museum of art with an extensive collection of modern artwork.

Strijp-S Community Gardens: Green areas where residents engage in urban farming and neighborhood activities are known as Strijp-S Community Gardens.

Useful apps and websites

Planning for Transportation:

- Google Maps app
- Website for public transportation: 9292 Journey Planner

Help with Language:

- Application: Duolingo (found in all major app shops)
- Website: Forvo (phrase pronunciation guide)

Local Festivals & Events:

- Meetup app (Excellent in the major app stores)
- Website: Meetup (find events near you)

Investigating Cuisine:

- TripAdvisor app (Excellent in the major app stores)

- Website: IENS (reviews and bookings for local restaurants)

Emergency Services Lookup:

- Application: SOS Emergency (available on all major app shops)
- Website: 112 Netherlands (emergency services information)

Local News and Updates:

- App: Nu.nl (Available on major app stores).
- Website: Eindhoven News (English-language local news)

Sustainable Events and Shopping:

- Download the Too Good To Go app from the main app stores.
- FeelGood Market (a local sustainable market) Website

Finance and Local Currency:

- Download the XE Currency Converter app from one of the main app stores.
- Website: ING Bank (for exchanging currencies)

Information for Travelers:

- App: Check Out Eindhoven (Excellent in the major app stores)
- Visit Eindhoven, the official city guide, on the internet

Outdoor Recreation and Exploration of Nature:

- App: AllTrails; accessible through the main app stores
- Website: Natuurmonumenten (activities and nature reserves)

Updates on the local weather:

- The Weather Channel app is accessible on most major app stores.
- Website for local weather forecasts: www.weeronline.nl

Cultural and Creative Findings:

- Van Abbemuseum App: accessible through the major app stores
- Van Abbemuseum website (exhibitions and museum information)

May these links and information be your compass as you explore the treasures of Eindhoven; a city that surprises around every corner. Eindhoven welcomes you with open arms and a wealth of experiences, whether your goals are exploring the city's technical hub, tasting regional specialties, or delving into creative treasures. May your trip to Eindhoven be nothing short of remarkable and safe travels!

Printed in Great Britain
by Amazon